A Note to Parents

DK READERS is a compelling program for beginning readers, designed in conjunction with leading literacy experts, including Dr. Linda Gambrell, Distinguished Professor of Education at Clemson University. Dr. Gambrell has served as President of the National Reading Conference, the College Reading Association, and the International Reading Association.

Beautiful illustrations and superb full-color photographs combine with engaging, easy-to-read stories to offer a fresh approach to each subject in the series. Each DK READER is guaranteed to capture a child's interest while developing his or her reading skills, general knowledge, and love of reading.

The five levels of DK READERS are aimed at different reading abilities, enabling you to choose the books that are exactly right for your child:

Pre-level 1: Learning to read
Level 1: Beginning to read
Level 2: Beginning to read alone
Level 3: Reading alone
Level 4: Proficient readers

The "normal" age at which a child begins to read can be anywhere from three to eight years old. Adult participation through the lower levels is very helpful for providing encouragement, discussing storylines, and sounding out unfamiliar words.

No matter which level you select, you can be sure that you are helping your child learn to read, then read to learn!

LONDON, NEW YORK, MUNICH,
MELBOURNE, and DELHI

DK LONDON
Series Editor Deborah Lock
US Senior Editor Shannon Beatty
Production Editor Francesca Wardell
Illustrator Vladimir Aleksic

Reading Consultant
Linda Gambrell, Ph.D.

DK DELHI
Editor Pomona Zaheer
Art Editors Shruti Soharia Singh, Jyotsna
DTP Designer Anita Yadav
Picture Researcher Aditya Katyal
Deputy Managing Editor Soma B. Chowdhury

First American Edition, 2014
Published in the United States by DK Publishing
345 Hudson Street, New York, New York 10014

14 15 16 17 18 10 9 8 7 6 5 4 3 2 1
001—197319—02/14

A catalog record for this book is available
from the Library of Congress.

ISBN: 978-1-4654-1721-3 (Paperback)
ISBN: 978-1-4654-1606-3 (Hardcover)

DK books are available at special discounts when
purchased in bulk for sales promotions, premiums,
fund-raising, or educational use.
For details, contact:
DK Publishing Special Markets
345 Hudson Street, New York, New York 10014
SpecialSales@dk.com

Printed and bound in China by
South China Printing Company

The publisher would like to thank the following for
their kind permission to reproduce their photographs:
(Key: a=above, b=below/bottom, c=center, l=left, r=right, t=top)
1 Dreamstime.com: Ayzek09 (c). **20–21 Dreamstime.com:**
Sarah2 (Reproduced Eleven Times). **22 Dorling Kindersley:**
Musee de Saint Malo, France (ca).
28 Dorling Kindersley: Musee de Saint Malo, France (b).
29 Dorling Kindersley: Musee de Saint Malo, France (c, cl).
32 Dorling Kindersley:
Musee de Saint Malo, France (c)
Jacket images: All cover images © Dorling Kindersley
All other images © Dorling Kindersley Limited
For further information see: www.dkimages.com

Discover more at
www.dk.com

BEGINNING
TO READ

1

Pirate Attack!

Written by Deborah Lock

"Ahoy there!
I am Jim, the cabin boy.
My ship is
the *Queen Anne's Revenge*.
So, you want to be a pirate.
Are you brave?
Do you love gold?
Yes? Then welcome aboard."

I will show you around the ship!

Hi, I am Polly!

"Heave ho!
We are loading up
food and weapons.
Can you pick up
this last crate
of pistols?
Follow me up
the gangplank."

weapon

"Here is Captain Blackbeard.
He is the meanest pirate ever.
He carries six pistols.
See that black smoke
all around his head?
He ties strings to his hair
and sets them on fire."

Wanted Dead or Alive!

Edward Teach
Known as Blackbeard the Pirate

Reward: 50 gold coins
(Beware! He is very dangerous.)

"Lift the anchor!" says
Captain Blackbeard.

anchor

The anchor is lifted.

"Hoist the sails."

The sails are raised.

The wind blows the sails

and the ship sets off.

"There is no getting off," says Jim.

"You are one of us now."

Hoist the sails!
Hoist the sails!

Here is Cook.
"Ahoy there,
stranger!"

"Have you come to help me
in the galley?" asks Cook.
"Taste my chicken bone soup.
Some more salt might make it
taste better!
This is the last of the chickens.
We will be eating
hard tack biscuits until
we catch our next turtle."

cutlass

"We cannot stand around
chatting in the galley," says Jim.
"There is work to be done
on the deck.

Sharpen the cutlasses.
Scrub the decks.

Shall we sing a sea shanty while
we work, my lads?
Strike up the drums and fiddles."

"Let us climb the rigging.
Check that the knots
on the ropes are tight.
We are very high.
We can see
a long way from here.
Sail, ho!
There is another ship."

knot

"All hands on deck,"
cries Captain Blackbeard.
"Let us join the others," says Jim.
The pirates vote to follow
and then attack the ship.
"Make ready!"
shouts Captain Blackbeard.
"Get your weapons ready,"
says Jim.
"You will need:

a pistol,

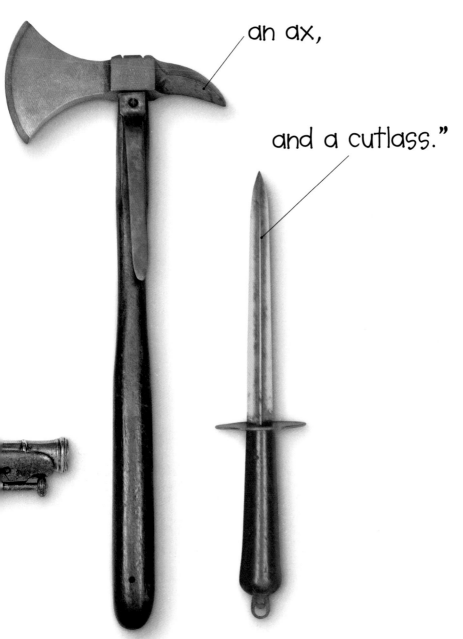

an ax,

and a cutlass."

The ship sails closer and closer.
"Hoist the Jolly Roger!"
shouts Captain Blackbeard.
"The flag shows that
we are pirates," says Jim.

Bang!

"Do not jump.
That was the cannon shot
to warn the other ship's crew.
Will they give us their gold
without a fight?"

"They do not.
Get ready to attack!
Raise the red flag.
We fight to the death.

Throw hooks to pull
the ships together.
Swing across from the rigging.
Then, fight with all you have got.

Hooray! We have won."

"What a great battle!
We take the gold.
Oh no!
The storm clouds are coming.
Those waves are huge."

Whoosh!

"Hold on!
Our ship will be smashed
if we hit a rock."

25

The sea is calm again.

"Land ahoy!" cries a pirate.

"There is our island," says Jim.

"We will sail around to the bay

so that we cannot be seen."

Splash!

The anchor is lowered.
We follow a map of the island
to find a treasure chest.
We dig down and pull it up.

treasure

Captain Blackbeard unlocks
the chest and lifts the lid.
The gems sparkle inside.
"We are rich!" shout the pirates.
Every pirate will have his share.
"Come and join the pirate party,"
says Jim.
"Yo ho ho!
It is a pirate's life for you
and me!"

Glossary

Anchor
something heavy used to stop the ship from moving

Cutlass
short sword with a curved blade

Knot
tying together pieces of material

Treasure
pile of gems and other objects that cost a lot

Weapon
tool used for fighting, such as a pistol

Index

DK READERS help children learn to read, then read to learn. If you enjoyed this DK READER, then look out for these other titles ideal for your child.

Level 1 Deadly Dinosaurs
Roar! Thud! Meet Rexy, Sid, Deano, and Sonia, the dinosaurs that come alive at night in the museum. Who do you think is the deadliest?

Level 1 LEGO® Legends of Chima™: Tribes of Chima
Enter the mysterious land of Chima™ and discover the amazing animal tribes who live there. Meet the Ravens, the Gorillas, the Eagles, the Crocodiles, the Lions, and the Wolves. But beware! Are they friends or foes?

Level 2 The Great Panda Tale
The zoo is getting ready to welcome a new panda baby. Join the excitement as Louise tells of her most amazing summer as a member of the zoo crew. What will the newborn panda look like?